The Paul Bunyan Ballroom
Bud Backen

Nixes Mate Books
Allston, Massachusetts

Copyright © 2017 Bud Backen

Book design by d'Entremont
Photo from the collection of Lauren Leja.

All rights reserved. This book or any portion thereof may not be reproduced or used in any manner whatsoever without the express written permission of the publisher except for the use of brief quotations in a book review or scholarly journal.

Special thanks to Ron Androla/Pressure Press & all my friends otherwise not mentioned.

ISBN 978-0-9991882-6-2

Nixes Mate Books
POBox 1179
Allston, MA 02134
nixesmate.pub/books

This book is for Molly

Contents

I saw	1
violet sunrise	2
hard to get	3
aqua blizzard	4
it was 200 feet down	6
I drive to work	7
2 a.m outskirts of wichita	8
so scared of living i'm afraid to die rag	10
topical poem	12
the crux	13
those days	14
turtle lake road	15
elia ericson	16
the snow	18
there's nobody up	19
she's still here	20
stripper	21
her magazine husband	22

shy	23
shotzy's	24
the atomic implosion of radio waves	26
young november moon	28
the paul bunyan ballroom	29
lake effect	30
high jinx	32
mudlarks	34
the cast iron cold	35
hard pressed	36
a phosphorous wind	38
last time	40
fly swatter	42
i've said it before	44
thicket	45
turns out	46
cabbage crop	48
the devil	50

The Paul Bunyan Ballroom

I saw

the soldier sky
marching across the moon
silent trumpets blaring inside the cloudbanks
like bombs bursting on the south ridge
destroying every town & family
w/a brutal fist of wind
meanwhile the mercury stars high above
sugared the fog blowing beneath a great
gray whale of darkness moving like a
stealthy black wildcat
rumbling like a menacing army running
straight towards the heart of town
nothing that fast takes long to pass
I watched it all from a lawn chair
seemed it rolled out of the west
but another wind squared it
lengthwise like a dead end cross
& a dark & dangerous jesus

violet sunrise

we slept in the hay
w/eight purring kittens
I woke w/the first
light breaking on the
edge of the loft
I drowsed in future
days ahead viewing
myself on the other
side of tomorrow
still vagrant or going
back from where I came
I woke again
now the sun
was raining in the
opened hay door
I noticed I was alone
aside from the cats
so I laid a while
packed up & hitched
to the interstate

hard to get

a good deal
everythings's a ripoff
cutting corners
on the cheap
smaller & more expensive
it's getting tiring
& I'm about to advance
I'm gonna sell robot parts
future clothes & ray guns
trips to other planets
insurance for your pets
cars that run on coffee
instead of gas
x-ray glasses
& grass
I'm gonna run for office
any office will do
as long as it has a window
& a washroom w/a view

aqua blizzard

made a
mess of things
the ache from
shoveling
carving through
four feet of snow
once more this
lifetime
tomorrow
they say more
maybe a foot
with winds
causing
serious drifting
there is no one
to challenge it
nobody going
nowhere &
it knows
so it blows
w/out restraint
or conscience
I call work

linda made it in
so did rick
but that won't
last long
they're closing
the town down
anybody out
there is at his
or her own
risk

it was 200 feet down

& 20 below zero
my fingers & toes
already numb
when I got a nosebleed
the air rescue crashed
into the mountainside
when I woke up
I bounced off the walls
to the bath
in the mirror I saw
myself as I really was –
bed-headed & ugly
recovering from near
death
I went back to sleep
& dreamt I was bowling
in a juke joint somewhere
I've never been but felt
right at home in & the
woman I know from the
gyro kiosk was there
but wasn't bowling
only sitting on my lap
making me need to pee

I drive to work

in a blue collar bustle
jammed up on route 22
always stalled by the
blatantly long lights on
kenwood & plathe
I hate every day i
take that way instead
of the bridge over the
river by the paper mill
where the stink is enough
to make you wish you
were dead & I always do
but it's not the stench
just the feeling I get that
almost 50 people that i
knew at one time or another
had to work inside that
smell & live to tell it
wasn't me though
I ran away
found any
other
job

2 a.m
outskirts of
wichita

exit 142 exxon
I gotta pee
gas up
keep going
try to reach
denver
by noon
lost the time
of day in a fog
visibility two
maybe
twenty feet
sometimes another
car would appear
like a smudged
polaroid & vanish
in muddy
wash water
utah
surreal & selfless
in its formations

& buttes
& salt
then nevada
then rolling
sierra madre
breaking a
continental
pledge to the
pacific shelf
to never shift
until it is time
arrived by the
morning after
w/a slight
heartache

so scared of living
i'm afraid to die rag

most terrible part
of winning
is losing it all –
what drives competition,
compels success.
shoulder to shoulder they march
toward an ecstasy ordained
by the holy wrath itself,
building a better world
through the taking
of all that's there
no matter whatever
stands in the way
& selling it.
when men don't
have the money
they suffer the cost;
whatever can't be
paid in cash
comes out of the flesh.
weather will turn
into a blueprint of

death, the oceans rise
winds blow away the
skies, the mood of the
moon will deteriorate
despite all the wishing
on all the stars,
& prayers to
the cloud gods above.
run away,
drive away,
fly away, all
ending up at the
same tired grave.

topical poem

a moonlit
van reflects a
single tooth
of the moon
into my bath
bouncing off
the medicine
cabinet mirror
& onto my
bloated thigh
sitting in
the night
maintaining
the dignity of
depositing my
waste in the
quiet of the dark
seated like
a real man

the crux

living in
dust to
share a
lasting
peace
bones
skin
heart
center
of light
pressing
toward
solitude
one or
two alone
together
beside a
fiery star
eloped
in death
forever

those days

humping
icy roads
to save us
from being
alone
to illuminate
dark thoughts
of umbra dreams
& suffocation
the brutal
mood of being
on the roof of
our souls w/out
a ladder

turtle lake road

elbows at the bridge
you gotta slow down
or you go right in the river
happened to shorty & bob
w/his GTO he got from his pa
for goin' to nam
ed's wrecker service
had to hoist it sideways
up the rocky ledge
ripping up the door panels
& fenders on the driver's side
but otherwise…
sheriff turner took a half hour
writing a ticket the whole time
explaining why the slow down
sign is there in the first place
but by then it didn't matter
no more

elia ericson

won the ticket to vegas
in the christmas lotto
at her job in the hair salon
down in the south side
next to sluggo's bar & grill
where they used to sell furniture
when I was a kid in the fifties
the deal was she had to take
the bus from omaha to reno
so bill the owner had to drive
her to the bus on his one day off
but didn't make it back in time
for the kids from the east side
to break through the washroom
window & try to blow open
the little safe behind bill's
desk next to the coke machine
in the back of the salon
the partition still needed
to be installed for the tenth
year straight but would've
had to be replaced after the
explosion ripped all the way

through the building killing
the poor little bastards
in their tracks but leaving
the safe intact
elia claimed it was all her fault
if bill had been there instead of
giving her a ride to omaha
the dead kids from the east
side would never have tried to
rob the place & that's when
bill told her to shut up

the snow

comes like mice
whitening the night
falling from mousy clouds
into a carpet of pillowy rice
bloodless & deepening
in piles
blowing a vortex
in the catcall-winds
chills from a leak in space
support a theory of climate change
as the ice collects & continues to haunt
months that passed since
the sun had a hand
in frightening the frostbite
of frigidity to her knobby
frozen knees
there is no words for it beyond
the land of frozen feet
& loveless overcast storms
inside a hell w/no heat

there's nobody up

when I walk
in the dark night
I see star's light
cold & uncaring
in their frozen stare
cross paths w/deer
together in this
nocturnal eminence
sharing our secrets
in startling suspicions

she's still here

in the corners
atop the tables
running laps around the living room
flying
no more need for food or water
the idyllic pet
superior
to the preverbal ten to twenty
year hitch comes w/hunger
thirst & a good place to
sleep...
the eternal relationship
nothing else in the universe
is better at
promises kept
nothing more true
than a good pet

stripper

lucy lynne she called herself
friends called her lucky
she was pretty &
her soul redeemed by jesus
had a cross tattoo on her left breast
another one below her navel
wasn't for my savior I'd be dead she sd
now I have eternal life
her show was ten sharp weeknights
I showed up late
she was down to her little loin cloth
covering up her tonto
life is a roller coaster ride she sd
until it aint
a few young christian college boys
hooted & clapped as she danced to
disco queen grinding her hips close
so the boys could stuff dollars in
her g-string
I always felt jealous

her magazine husband

lifted his drink
called for his putter
the one he named rose
I remember him
at the cabin
w/his little red car
fastest in the county
so claimed all his
pretentious buddies he
hung with in town
at the all night café
out by route 9
rowdy bunch w/nothing
to do & nowhere to
bring it
till they were 21 & the
only one who already was
is eddy who got drafted
this summer at the fair
we met some girls from fargo
said they knew elvis
said he was a fag

shy

she worked at astro's
I didn't care for the burgers there
the buns were powdery & dry
fell apart when you held it too tight
but she was a beauty beyond compare
I wondered what happened that
drove her there
serving burgers w/powder buns
& pretty darn good onion rings
I struggled w/the idea of knowing her
introducing myself between bites
when she dropped by to ask if everything
is alright I'd tell her it might be better if
I could buy her a burger
but I never did
never went back
something told me
if I got too close
& tried anything
someone would
shoot me

shotzy's

biker bar
littered w/harleys
all summer long
sherman lindy
among them
an old friend
divorced my
high school
sweetheart for
his love of the
open road
forty years on
ended up on this
side of town
bartending at
shotzy's then
found himself
married to
sugar bear larson
who owns half the
ginny's chicken stops
in town got them
from her pa

who aggrandized
the working man
w/an honest wage
a week off paid
& a raise
for every year
of service

the atomic implosion of radio waves

the old tube radio in eddy's '55 buick
could bring in japan sometimes if the
moon was rising full that summer us guys
liked to listen to little rock late drinking beer
& laughing one night I bumped the channel
changer & some guy was talking about jesus
we listened unable to turn it off
it was about how god said in revelation
there would be a calling out of those
that are good & bad & the judgement
should separate us like wheat from the
chaff it was the night eddy told us he
was gonna sell the buick & buy a brand
new chevette if his old man would
co-sign we were driving home & they
played satisfaction & it felt like the
first time so I turned it up & belched
the stones are jesus eddy said
I agreed got out at my house
watched him drive away listening to
the dynaflow transmission pull
eddy home up the street to his drunken
sleep we'd be lucky if his new chevette

radio could haul in des moines or even
minneapolis but it didn't matter
school was about to start again &
nothing really helped

young november moon

splays across the room in grace
a presence pervades to pray for me
outward to the holy atomic structure
& the gods of matter that threaten to
sink the ship of state
if we don't decide to
divide the booty evenly
or go down in shame
meanwhile
scoundrels precipitate the lawn of
the west wing the great overture
of the ramrod king surges through
the air like a bad dream
money works in the kitchen now
we eat until we die

the paul bunyan ballroom

was on highway 169 at the
junction of county 14
saturday nights they had a
local hootenanny featuring
all the yocals that came in
from the farms & townships
surrounding the entire limp
lake area plus the next county
south heard about it & there
was always their jugband
showing up
the paul bunyan ballroom
burned down in '92 after a
lightning storm ignited the
power pole behind the barn
& the whole place went up
anyway that's where I met
ramona one night outside
smokin' she wasn't married
but about to & I had a hint
it wouldn't matter if she did
or didn't but found out later
she did

lake effect

the sun's out.
clouds tucked it under
for over a week.
millie stopped by
to wisen me
an eclipse will
sweep the nation clean
of those vermin men
that blow
themselves up
big as giants
with germy words.
what flowers to
plant that deer won't
devour is my concern.
millie thinks I need to
pull my head out of
my ass & smell the
roses
when it occurs to me
why there's thorns;
it's not because love is
prickly & painful,

it's to keep the deer
from eating their buds
or there'd be no
roses at all.

high jinx

the river by my house feeds
the entire st.lawrence seaway
but you couldn't tell by looking
at it
seems to be more like a pretty
lake w/a little island in the middle
one day a kid thought it would
be fun to ride his bike down the
hill that leads to the landing
& off the dock into the water
they found the bike but
never saw the boy again
this is thirteen years since
there's a current there down deep
can take things a thousand miles
dump 'em into the atlantic ocean
w/out surfacing once
it's a force just put there
by something I'd hate to
rattle too much
last summer I sat on that dock
dangled my feet in the water
thought about things passing by

deep down in the current
whole trees rocks the size of me
entire cliff-sides deer dogs cats
ermine little boys

mudlarks

sat on horse back
fetching flies & gnats
feasting on a host of things
when the wind died down
we was all out back
listening to the graybills sing
a west wind filled the aspens
on the vacant mountainside
groomed for skiers
clumps of pine & willow
stood dancing in the breeze
humming a back-up song
I thought I was in love
but she left w/some hippie
who drove a blue subaru
I couldn't compete having
just hitched in & didn't
know anyone
I left the next day & wondered
if those folks felt any envy
at how I could just walk off

the cast iron cold

january spits a frozen mist
on the windshield of my car
defrost creates a hole about
the size of my fist to see the
road ahead the windshield
wash will defrost everything
for only a few seconds but
that's enough to move forward
another quarter mile w/out
too much ado the worse it gets
the oncoming headlights blind
the works I'm hopefully not
heading into the ditch
I got Sibelius on the classical
radio calming my angry spirit
mad at winter again cussing
& demanding justice for this
crime of agony & frozen blood
frosted lungs tanned cheeks
& hands cold cold feet & ears
blackened from a frostbiting
bitch w/no respect for any life

hard pressed

she was elevated w/high heels
looking me in the eyes
created a friction throughout the
dance especially when she started
making eyes at the blue suit
I wanted to be anywhere else
so I called a cab & snuck out the
back door by the restrooms
outside the air was warm
all of summer lay ahead
cab took me to the bloodshot bar
twice the fun & half the class
as the drab old wedding dance
next day she called while
I brushed my teeth asked
what happened so I told her
I felt ill at ease & hard pressed
to stay at the dance
so I went outside for
some air & it was so sweet
I fell asleep over by a hedge
of bougainvillea & when I woke
it was nearly dawn

then why did jane wadsworth
tell me about you asking her
for a date last night at the bloodshot
bar & how come you lie to me
I hung up the phone & waddled into
the kitchen to see if there was
some way of recovering from any of this
w/food

a phosphorous wind

white w/mist & thick
like smoky fire
a road flows west &
south again after it
crosses train tracks
follows the rainy river
to maddog flats

wasn't this time of year
closer to spring with
yellow blossoms on
almost everything
else it was white
the only other color

nanette miller said
she set her barn ablaze
but everyone knew
she didn't that barn
still stands today
if you want to go look

it was lies like that set her
apart from other gals
why I married her & we
drove clear to the columbia
heights exit before i realized
we forgot the dog

last time

I was ever at a dime
store picking up a few
quick christmas presents

at the checkout was
a rack of rabbit's foots
on little silver chains

the big week past fast
mama shone bright as
the christmas tree

lipstick red as the nose
on the rudolph reindeer
eyeshadow matched me

a wreath hung high up
on the front porch door
like a hopeful sign on

an empty scoreboard
was going to give mama
the rabbit's foot but

I liked the bracelet with
pretty pearls more so i
gave her that

kept the rabbit's foot for
my own good luck &
future soul but I lost it

fly swatter

hung from a nail
next to the stove
in eddy's kitchen
in the bath
the seat for the
toilet leaned against
the wall in case
you needed it
his back yard was
an alley
his mailbox
an old bucket
w/a lid in case
of rain
he made good
money teaching physics
at the college
it's just that
he never really came
back from iraq
hated himself
& there was no cure
except poverty

& self abuse
until one day he
met amy
everything seemed
repaired
for about a month
then he shot himself

i've said it before

but i should get paid
for feeding these birds
it's a service i provide
keeping them healthy
making them happy
so they stick around
after all what kind of a
world would it be w/out
birds I swear every time
i think – oh – here comes
my friend cindy who works
for the jehovah witnesses
she likes to argue about god

thicket

by the sidewalk
grew there by itself
long as I left it alone
quit mowing over it
one day I said to myself
I wonder what that is
don't look like grass
got curious enough
to just leave it alone
let it be what it is
now it sprouts berries
for the birds & squirrels
to eat before the claw
of winter scrapes every
last scrap of nourishment
leaving the thicket looking
like a briar stick bush of
the witch that eats children

turns out

I aint doing my
laundry right
found out last night

women who don't
mean to can sometimes
mean a lot

she says how do you
add soap to your machine
& when I told her she

laughed at me called
me a man about it
you men she said

don't know shit about
what counts the most
look at yourself

it was then I noticed
the dinge around my
cuffs the ring around

the collar I'd heard so
much about through
my entire life

made me feel responsible
to get wedded at some point
get out there & find her
somewhere

I'll know her by the
whiteness of her whites
& the deeper colors
of her deepest darks

cabbage crop

weather bit the corn
dried up the carrots
should've moved to
someplace wet after
the war grandpa
always said but who
listened & now this
they're foreclosing
on the land he bought
w/the money he took
for killing as many
folks as he could back
in the war to end all
wars way before we was
born

across the road you
can hear the neighbor
girls sing while they
swing & laugh
it's carried on the
breeze that is killing
the hay that drowned

last may in the flood
that got us trapped
on the roof of the barn
that we tore down
cause it rotted at the
foundation

yesterday another crow
lay dead by the fence
like his last thought was
flying away if only
he could make it to the
sky

the devil

rides in a blue blazer
selling bar supplies
eating burgers from
any drive-thru window
living on a commission
he needs a raise
to feed the kids
since his wife ran off
w/the middle class
mailman

whatever justice
there is in a world
where the devil
takes his licks in
a slave's paycheck
is alright with him

he's really just in it
for the ride
the devil likes to
drive the highways
reminds him of

how a straight
line can suddenly
take a lazy curve
& turn it all into
good intentions

About the Author

Bud Backen lives alone, low-income & healthy. Works hard doing menial cleaning at a local bakery. Writes for fun & otherwise likes to walk & sometimes wishes he had someone to talk to. But not often since he has little to talk about that isn't abstract & confusing to anyone w/real sense.

Nixes Mate Books features small-batch artisanal literature, created by writers that use all 26 letters of the alphabet and then some, honing their craft the time-honored way: one line at a time.

More Nixes Mate titles:
ON BROAD SOUND | Rusty Barnes
KINKY KEEPS THE HOUSE CLEAN | Mari Deweese
SQUALL LINE ON THE HORIZON | Pris Campbell
COMES TO THIS | Jeff Weddle
HITCHHIKING BEATITUDES | Michael McInnis
AIR & OTHER STORIES | Lauren Leja
WAITING FOR AN ANSWER | Heather Sullivan
A WORLD WHERE | Paul Brookes
MY SOUTHERN CHILDHOOD | Pris Campbell

Forthcoming titles from Nixes Mate:
NIXES MATE REVIEW ANTHOLOGY 2016/17
CAPP ROAD | Matt Borczon
LUBBOCK ELECTRIC | Anne Elezabeth Pluto
WAR IN THE TIME OF LOVE | Michael McInnis

nixesmate.pub/books

www.ingramcontent.com/pod-product-compliance
Lightning Source LLC
Chambersburg PA
CBHW052136010526
44113CB00036B/2276